SNOW LEOPARDS

by Lucia Raatma

Children's Press®

An Imprint of Scholastic Inc.
New York Toronto London Auckland Sydney
Mexico City New Delhi Hong Kong
Danbury, Connecticut

Content Consultant
Dr. Stephen S. Ditchkoff
Professor of Wildlife Sciences
Auburn University
Auburn, Alabama

Library of Congress Cataloging-in-Publication Data
Raatma, Lucia.
  Snow leopards / by Lucia Raatma.
    pages cm.—(Nature's children)
  Includes bibliographical references and index.
  ISBN 978-0-531-23362-7 (lib. bdg.) – ISBN 978-0-531-25160-7 (pbk.)
1. Snow leopard—Juvenile literature. I. Title.
  QL737.C23R237 2013
  599.75'54—dc23   2013000095

Snow Leopards

Class	Mammalia
Order	Carnivora
Family	Felidae
Genus	*Panthera*
Species	*Panthera uncia*
World distribution	The mountains of central Asia
Habitat	Primarily found along the cliffs and rocky slopes of some of the highest mountains in the world
Distinctive physical characteristics	Thick fur with gray and black markings that provide camouflage; tails that are nearly as long as their bodies; short ears and muzzle
Habits	Territorial; nomadic; provide care for cubs for first two years of life; active at night; mate during winter
Diet	Blue sheep and ibex; smaller animals such as birds, marmots, and rabbits

Contents

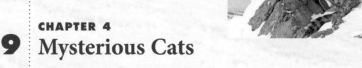

CHAPTER 1

All About Snow Leopards

Thousands of feet above sea level, a small team of scientists made camp for the night. They had climbed the slopes of the world's tallest mountain, Mount Everest, in search of the mysterious snow leopard. Snow leopards are very good at staying out of sight, and their total population in the wild is very small. As a result, this remarkable cat is rarely seen in the wild.

Just after sunset, the scientists began to hear distressed sounds coming from a nearby herd of ibex. They looked at each other, knowing that the noises could only mean one thing. With cameras in hand, they crept toward the ibex. Along the edges of the herd, the scientists saw the outline of a large, spotted cat. They snapped pictures as the snow leopard hungrily eyed the goats. The trip was a success! The scientists were thrilled to be one of the few groups to have ever laid eyes on this remarkable animal.

Because snow leopards are secretive and live in places where it is difficult to travel, humans rarely see them.

Lengthy Leopards

Snow leopards are considered medium-size wild cats. Most snow leopards weigh between 60 and 120 pounds (27 and 54 kilograms), and they are about 24 inches (61 centimeters) tall at the shoulder. Males are between 39 and 51 inches (99 and 130 cm) long, measuring from the nose to the base of the tail. Females are slightly smaller, measuring 31 to 39 inches (79 to 99 cm) long on average.

Snow leopards' tails are between 31 and 39 inches (79 and 99 cm) long. That is almost as long as their bodies. A snow leopard uses its tail for balance as it makes its way through rugged terrain. The tail is covered with thick fur, so the cat uses it like a blanket. A snow leopard will wrap its tail around its body to stay warm in the cold weather.

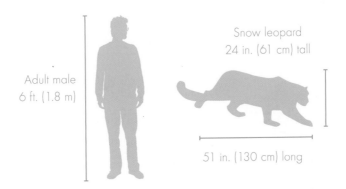

Adult male
6 ft. (1.8 m)

Snow leopard
24 in. (61 cm) tall

51 in. (130 cm) long

A snow leopard's long body helps it stalk prey.

High-Up Habitats

Snow leopards live in the mountains of central Asia. Their habitat runs through 12 countries, including Bhutan, China, India, Nepal, Pakistan, Russia, and Mongolia. The total range of the snow leopard's habitat is more than 1.2 million square miles (3.1 million square kilometers). This is about one-third the size of the United States.

One of the mountain ranges where snow leopards live is the Himalayas. This range has some of the tallest mountains in the world, including Mount Everest, which is the world's highest peak at 29,035 feet (8,850 meters) tall. Snow leopards climb high up into these mountains. During some parts of the year, they can be found living as high as 18,000 feet (5,486 m) above the ground.

FUN FACT! Some people in Asia refer to snow leopards as "ghost cats."

Snow leopards prefer steep slopes and mountainsides to flat, open spaces.

Built for the Cold

Snow leopards are well suited for surviving in their ice-cold homes. They are covered with fur that helps keep them warm. The fur on the bottom side of a snow leopard's body is particularly thick. This protects the cat's belly as it moves around close to the ground. A snow leopard's fur grows thicker when the weather gets colder. It also grows up to 4.5 inches (11 cm) longer.

The fur can be white, light yellow, or gray. It is covered in a pattern of gray and black spots called rosettes. Each cat has a unique arrangement of rosettes. The rosettes act as camouflage. They help make the leopard hard to see among the rocks and cliffs.

A snow leopard has a short nose, small ears, and a domed forehead. Its nasal passages and chest are large. This allows the leopard to breathe in large amounts of cold mountain air and warm it up.

Snow leopards are tough animals that can survive the harsh conditions of their mountain habitats.

CHAPTER 2

Surviving in the Snow

High up in the mountains, snow leopards are one of the top predators. They are not afraid to hunt and attack other animals. In fact, they face very few dangers in the wild.

Snow leopards are carnivores. This means they eat meat. Although they are not very big, snow leopards are very strong. They often hunt animals that are larger than they are. Their main sources of food are blue sheep and ibex. Blue sheep, also known as bharals, are found in the Himalaya mountain range. Ibex are a type of wild goat that lives in rugged mountains.

In addition, snow leopards often eat deer and wild pigs. They also feed on smaller animals such as birds, rabbits, and marmots. Along with meat, snow leopards also eat twigs and grass.

Snow leopards are capable of killing animals that are three times their size.

On the Prowl

Snow leopards hunt by hiding behind rocks and other parts of the terrain and waiting for the best time to launch a surprise attack. The coloring of their coats and spots helps them blend into the mountains. This means that other animals have a hard time seeing them. At the same time, snow leopards have a very easy time spotting their prey. They have excellent vision that is much better than a human's eyesight. They can even see well in low light, so they can hunt at night. Once snow leopards locate their prey, they usually jump down and attack the animal from above. If necessary, they will chase their prey down a mountainside until they catch it.

A snow leopard may spend three to four days eating a meal. During this time, it protects its catch from other animals. Snow leopards can go many days in between meals. A single blue sheep can provide enough food for a snow leopard to survive for two weeks.

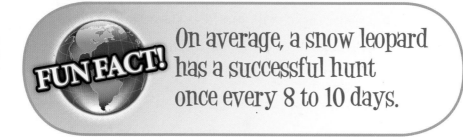

FUN FACT! On average, a snow leopard has a successful hunt once every 8 to 10 days.

Snow leopards must sometimes use their speed to catch fleeing prey.

Making a Move

Snow leopards live in rugged areas with high cliffs and sharp rocks. A human climbing a mountain would need ropes and other equipment. Snow leopards are naturally equipped to face the challenges of mountain climbing. They use their strong chests and long tails to help them balance on high cliffs. Their muscular shoulders help them climb and jump.

Snow leopards have very strong legs. Their front legs are shorter than their back legs. This makes it easier for them to run up and down steep slopes. Snow leopards also use their powerful legs to jump from cliff to cliff. They can jump as far as 40 feet (12 m) to attack their prey.

Snow leopards rely on their paws to get through snow and across rocky mountainsides. The fur underneath their paws provides cushion, which protects them from rough ground. It also provides traction in the snow. A snow leopard's paws are very wide. This allows the cat to walk on the surface of deep snow without falling through. A snow leopard can easily walk through snow as deep as 30 inches (76 cm).

A snow leopard's mighty leap helps it climb difficult terrain and attack prey.

Season to Season

As the seasons change, snow leopards move up and down the slopes of their mountain homes. The main reason they do this is to follow their prey. In spring, most of the animals that snow leopards prey on begin to move into higher parts of the mountains. The snow leopards follow. During the warmest months of summer, snow leopards climb high to elevations of up to about 18,000 feet (5,486 m). In fall, as the weather begins to cool down, the snow leopards' prey moves to lower elevations in the mountains. The cats follow then as well.

Winter is the most difficult season because the ground is completely covered by snow and ice. Hunting in deep snow is hard, so sometimes the cats cannot find food. As a result, snow leopards move even farther down the mountains during the coldest parts of the year to find prey and hunt more easily. In the winter months, they are mostly found at elevations of about 6,000 feet (1,829 m).

Snow leopards use their tails to help them balance as they climb along steep mountainsides.

CHAPTER 3

Leopard Life

Snow leopards do not live in large groups. Instead, they are solitary. They tend to live and hunt alone, away from one another. Snow leopards do not have permanent homes. They sleep in different places every night and often travel many miles every day in search of food.

Only during mating season are snow leopards social. Each mating season is about one week long. Mating season is usually in winter, sometime between January and March. During this time, snow leopards leave markings to attract mates. They leave scents or scrapes in the ground. They claw on big rocks and tree trunks. They may also leave their urine to show other snow leopards where they are.

Snow leopards sometimes communicate by hissing, growling, and mewing. During mating season, male and female snow leopards call to one another using a wailing sound.

A wide variety of sounds and facial expressions help snow leopards communicate with one another.

Snow Leopard Cubs

Soon after a male and a female snow leopard mate, the male leaves. The pregnant female begins looking for a location to give birth. She chooses a spot that is hidden and easy to defend from enemies who might want to harm her babies. About 100 days after mating, she is ready to produce a litter. Most snow leopard litters have two or three cubs. Because the father leaves before the litter is born, the mother snow leopard is left to raise her cubs on her own.

Snow leopard cubs are helpless when they are born. They weigh between 11 and 25 ounces (312 and 709 grams) at birth. They usually do not open their eyes until they are about a week old. In the first weeks of their life, they rely on their mother's milk for nutrition. As the cubs get older, the mother snow leopard begins providing them with meat from her kills.

Snow leopard cubs look adorable, but they soon grow to become ferocious hunters.

The Life Cycle

Mother snow leopards provide food and protection for their cubs for nearly two years, especially during their first winter. The cubs follow their mother and watch how she hunts. When the cubs are around two months old, they begin eating solid food. When they are three months old, they begin learning how to hunt. The young snow leopards finally begin to strike out on their own when they are 18 to 22 months old. By the time they are two to three years old, female snow leopards can begin producing litters of their own. Male snow leopards start mating by the time they are around four years old.

When they live in zoos or protected parks, snow leopards can live as long as 22 years. However, snow leopards face a more difficult life in the wild. They struggle to find food and avoid danger. Scientists estimate that most snow leopards live for 10 to 15 years in the wild.

Snow leopard mothers show affection for their cubs by licking them.

CHAPTER 4

Mysterious Cats

Because they are so rare and mysterious, snow leopards have captured human imaginations for thousands of years. Some people once believed that the cats were magical beings. Long ago in Nepal, people believed that snow leopards were sent by mountain gods to punish herders by killing their livestock. Other people told stories of religious leaders who took on the shape of snow leopards to travel through the wilderness.

As a result of stories like these, the snow leopard has become a popular symbol in many Asian countries. Old paper money from Kazakhstan also has an illustration of a snow leopard on it. The snow leopard is the symbol of the Girl Scouts Association in the nation of Kyrgyzstan.

The city of Almaty, Kazakhstan, includes a snow leopard in its official seal.

Learning About Leopards

Fossils tell us that snow leopards have been living on Earth for millions of years. However, it wasn't until 1970 that scientists obtained the first photographic proof that these incredible cats existed. That year, a scientist named Dr. George B. Schaller took what are believed to be the first photographs of snow leopards. The photos were published in *National Geographic* magazine in 1971.

Even today, it is difficult for scientists to study snow leopards. This is because the cats live in remote environments that are difficult to reach. Snow leopard sightings are also very rare. When people do manage to spot these cats, the snow leopards can quickly disappear because they are camouflaged by their fur coats.

To learn more about snow leopards, scientists have to be adventurers. They have to climb mountains and camp in the wild. Some spend weeks at a time in mountain environments in hopes of spotting a snow leopard in its natural habitat.

Even when they are not surrounded by snow, snow leopards can be extremely difficult to spot.

A Family of Felines

The snow leopard belongs to the family Felidae. This family is made up of all of the world's cat species, also known as felines. The earliest felines lived about 37 million years ago. Many of the earliest cat species were much larger than the ones living now. Today, there are 37 different feline species. Scientists divide them into two subfamilies.

The subfamily Felinae is made up of smaller cats. These include ocelots, bobcats, and caracals. They also include slightly larger cats such as cougars and cheetahs. Domestic house cats are a part of Felinae, too. The cats in Felinae are sometimes known as purring cats. This is because they do not make loud, roaring sounds. Instead, they produce purrs that their larger relatives cannot make. Unlike larger cats, Felinae cats have a rigid bone in their throats. The purring sound is produced by the vibration of this bone.

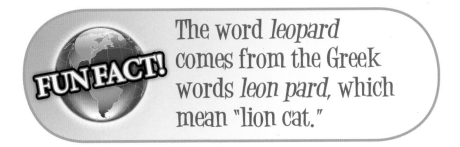

FUN FACT! The word *leopard* comes from the Greek words *leon pard*, which mean "lion cat."

Pet cats have many things in common with snow leopards.

Closest Cat Relatives

Snow leopards are part of the second Felidae subfamily, Pantherinae. This subfamily includes tigers, lions, jaguars, and leopards. These large hunters are known as the roaring cats. They are the snow leopard's closest relatives.

Though closely related, the leopard is not the same species as the snow leopard. Instead of gray fur, the leopard's upper body is covered in yellow fur and dark rosettes. It lives in forests throughout Africa and in parts of Asia. Like the snow leopard, it is an excellent hunter and a strong climber.

The tiger is the largest member of the Felidae family. An adult tiger can weigh as much as 660 pounds (300 kg). That is more than five times the size of a fully grown male snow leopard! Tigers are known for their orange fur and distinctive black stripes. Like other large cats, they are remarkable hunters. They mainly hunt large animals such as deer, but they also enjoy snacking on porcupines.

Tigers are found in many different habitats, including forests, swamps, and grasslands.

CHAPTER 5

Leopards in Jeopardy

Snow leopards are endangered. This means they are at risk of dying out forever. By some estimates, only 3,500 to 4,000 snow leopards are left in the wild. In addition, approximately 500 live around the world in zoos and wildlife parks. In these places, they are protected.

Humans are the biggest danger to snow leopards. One way people cause problems for these cats is by destroying their habitats. When people take over wild land to expand towns and farms, there is less room for wild animals to live and find food. Many of the animals that snow leopards prey on are left with nowhere to graze. As these animals die out or move to new homes, snow leopards are left with little to eat.

Climate change is another danger to snow leopards. As Earth gets warmer, the weather on the mountains changes. This can make the snow leopards' hunting ground much smaller. That may force the cats to move higher and higher up the mountains.

Zoos and wildlife parks provide the only opportunity most people will ever have to see a snow leopard up close.

Too Much Hunting

Even though snow leopards are endangered, some people continue to hunt them. One reason is that some people believe that a snow leopard's skin, bones, and other body parts have healing properties. In China, there is high demand for these body parts.

People also hunt snow leopards for their beautiful furs. The furs are used to create coats, hats, and other clothing. Even though the fur trade is harmful and illegal, many people still want to wear these clothes. Some people who live in central Asia are poor. Wealthy people will pay a lot of money for the furs, so poachers hunt snow leopards illegally to make a living.

Additionally, snow leopards are often killed by herders who want to protect their livestock. When snow leopards' normal prey becomes hard to find, the cats sometimes move closer to villages. There, they attack and eat cows and sheep.

Though it is illegal to hunt snow leopards in many parts of the world, some hunters cannot resist the temptation of killing them for their valuable fur.

Letting Leopards Live

The world's population of snow leopards is on the decline. If humans continue to hunt them and destroy habitats, these cats could one day be gone forever.

Some conservation groups are working to protect snow leopards. They are trying to mate the cats in zoos and wildlife parks so their numbers can grow. They are also trying to help the people of central Asia learn how to protect their livestock from snow leopards without killing the cats.

Some groups are encouraging tourists to visit Asia to try to see snow leopards in person. This raises awareness about the cats. It also brings more money to the people of Asia, who can be paid for services such as providing food and a place to stay. The more people know about these mysterious "ghost cats," the more they may want to help them.

Cubs born in zoos have longer life spans than those born in the wild.

Words to Know

camouflage (KAM-uh-flahzh) — a disguise or a natural coloring that allows animals, people, or objects to hide by making them look like their surroundings

carnivores (KAHR-nuh-vorz) — animals that eat meat

climate (KLYE-mut) — the weather typical of a place over a long period of time

conservation (kahn-sur-VAY-shuhn) — the protection of valuable things, especially forests, wildlife, natural resources, or artistic or historic objects

domestic (duh-MES-tik) — animals that have been tamed; people use domestic animals as a source of food or as work animals, or keep them as pets

elevations (el-uh-VAY-shuhnz) — heights above sea level

endangered (en-DAYN-jurd) — at risk of becoming extinct, usually because of human activity

fossils (FAH-suhlz) — bones, shells, or other traces of an animal or plant from long ago, preserved as rocks

graze (GRAYZ) — to feed on grass that is growing in a field

habitat (HAB-uh-tat) — the place where an animal or a plant is usually found

litter (LIT-ur) — a number of baby animals that are born at the same time to the same mother

mating (MAYT-ing) — joining together to produce babies

nasal (NAY-zuhl) — having to do with the nose

poachers (POH-churz) — people who hunt or fish illegally

predators (PRED-uh-turz) — animals that live by hunting other animals for food prey (PRAY) — an animal that's hunted by another animal for food

rosettes (roh-ZETS) — colored markings on an animal

solitary (SAH-luh-ter-ee) — not requiring or without the companionship of others

species (SPEE-sheez) — one of the groups into which animals and plants of the same genus are divided; members of the same species can mate and have offspring

terrain (tuh-RAYN) — an area of land

traction (TRAK-shuhn) — the force that keeps a moving body from slipping on a surface

Habitat Map

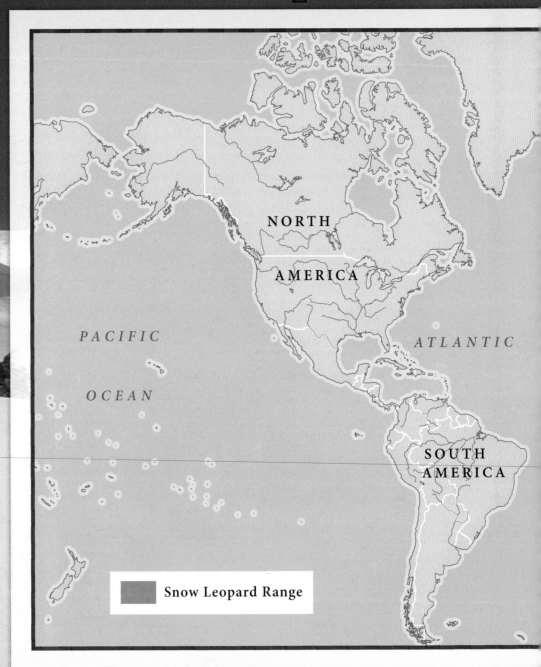

NORTH

AMERICA

PACIFIC

OCEAN

ATLANTIC

SOUTH
AMERICA

Snow Leopard Range

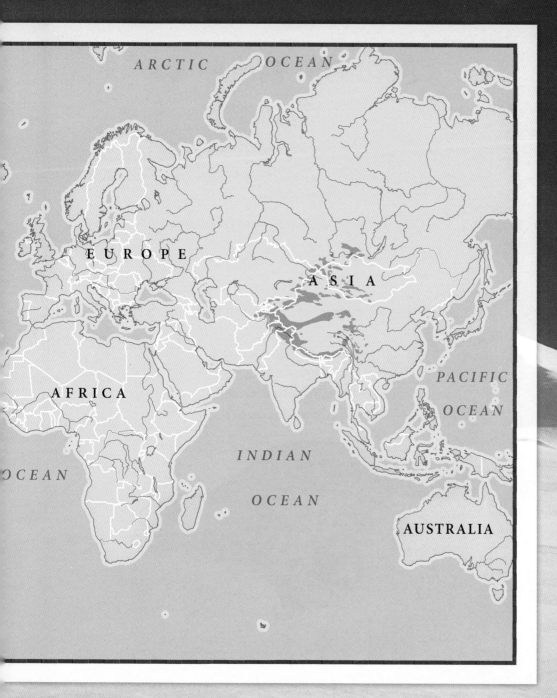

ARCTIC OCEAN

EUROPE

ASIA

AFRICA

PACIFIC OCEAN

OCEAN

INDIAN OCEAN

AUSTRALIA

Find Out More

Books

Fujita, Rima. *Save the Himalayas*. New York: One Peace Books, 2011.

Hatkoff, Juliana, Isabella Hatkoff, and Craig Hatkoff. *Leo the Snow Leopard: The True Story of an Amazing Rescue*. New York: Scholastic, 2010.

Landau, Elaine. *Snow Leopards: Hunters of the Snow and Ice*. Berkeley Heights, NJ: Enslow, 2010.

Visit this Scholastic Web site for more information on snow leopards:
www.factsfornow.scholastic.com
Enter the keywords **Snow Leopards**

Index

Page numbers in *italics* indicate a photograph or map.

About the Author

Lucia Raatma earned a bachelor's degree from the University of South Carolina and a master's degree from New York University. She has authored dozens of books for young readers, and she particularly enjoys writing about wildlife and conservation. She hopes that conservation groups are successful in their efforts to save snow leopards.